olivia rodrigo

ukulele

ISBN 978-1-70514-843-3

Visit Hal Leonard Online at
www.halleonard.com

Contact us:
Hal Leonard
7777 West Bluemound Road
Milwaukee, WI 53213
Email: info@halleonard.com

In Europe, contact:
Hal Leonard Europe Limited
42 Wigmore Street
Marylebone, London, W1U 2RN
Email: info@halleonardeurope.com

In Australia, contact:
Hal Leonard Australia Pty. Ltd.
4 Lentara Court
Cheltenham, Victoria, 3192 Australia
Email: info@halleonard.com.au

contents

Brutal

Words and Music by Olivia Rodrigo and Daniel Nigro

First note

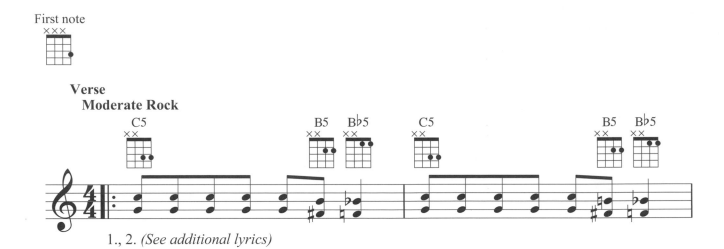

Verse
Moderate Rock

1., 2. *(See additional lyrics)*

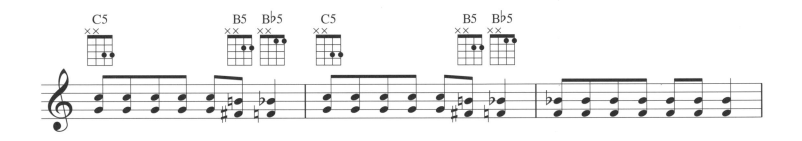

𝄋 Chorus

All I did was try my best, this the kind of thanks I get. ____

I'm re - lent - less - ly up - set. _____ They

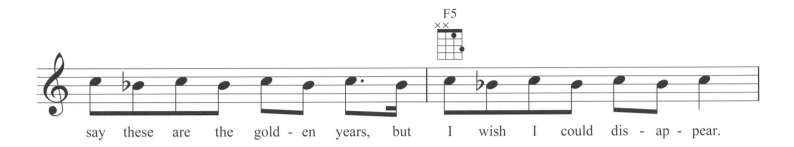

say these are the gold - en years, but I wish I could dis - ap - pear.

Interlude

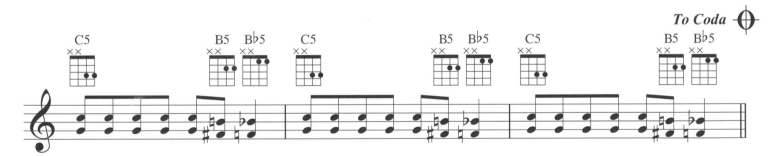

E - go crush is so se - vere. God, it's bru - tal out here. *(Instrumental)*

To Coda ⊕

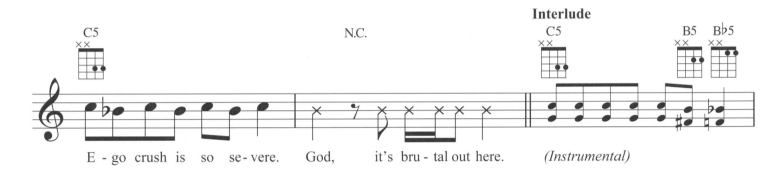

Verse

N.C.

3. *(See additional lyrics)*

D.S. al Coda

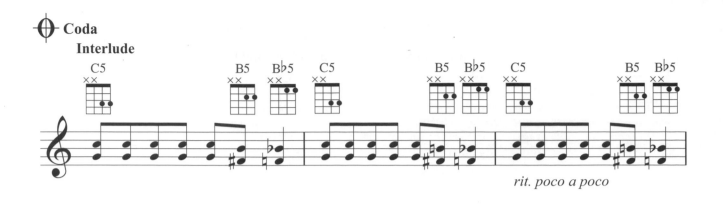

Coda

Interlude

rit. poco a poco

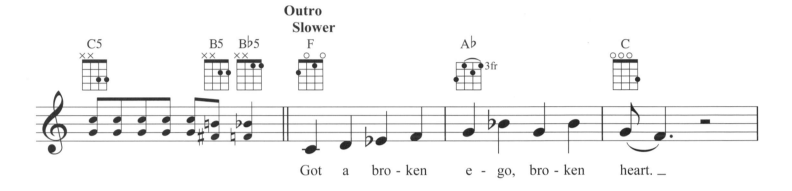

Outro

Slower

Got a bro-ken e-go, bro-ken heart. _

God, I don't e-ven know where to start.

Additional Lyrics

1. I'm so insecure, I think that I'll die before I drink.
   And I'm so caught up in the news of who likes me and who hates you.
   And I'm so tired that I might quit my job, start a new life.
   And they'd all be so disappointed 'cause who am I, if not exploited?

2. And I'm so sick of seventeen. I'm over this teenage dream.
   If someone tells me one more time, "Enjoy your youth," I'm gonna cry.
   And I don't stick up for myself, I'm anxious and nothing can help.
   And I wish I'd done this before. And I wish people liked me more.

3. I feel like no one wants me, and I hate the way I'm perceived.
   I only have two real friends, and lately I'm a nervous wreck.
   'Cause I love people I don't like, and I hate every song I write.
   And I'm not cool and I'm not smart, and I can't even parallel park.

Drivers License

Words and Music by Olivia Rodrigo and Daniel Nigro

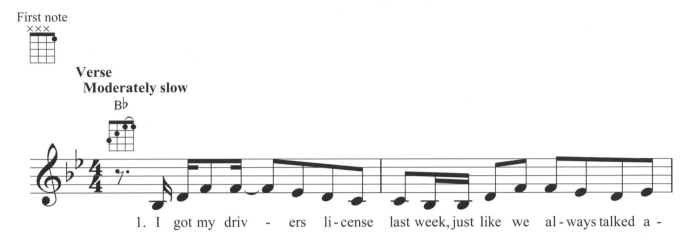

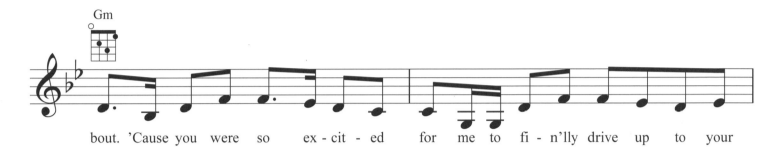

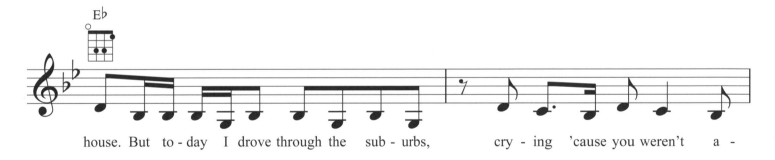

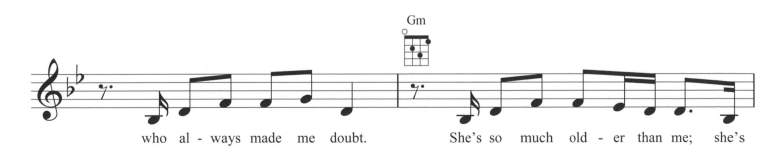

ev-'ry-thing I'm ___ in - se - cure a-bout. Yeah, to - day I drove through the sub - urbs,

'cause how could I ev - er love some - one else? And

𝄋 Chorus

I know we weren't per-fect, but I've nev - er felt this way for no one. And

I just can't i - mag - ine how you could be so o - kay ___ now that I'm ___

___ gone. { Guess }{ I guess } you did - n't mean what you wrote in that song a - bout

me. _____ 'Cause you said for - ev - er; now I drive a - lone past your

street. _____ 3. And all my friends are tired _____

of hear-ing how much I miss you; but I kind of feel sor - ry for them, 'cause

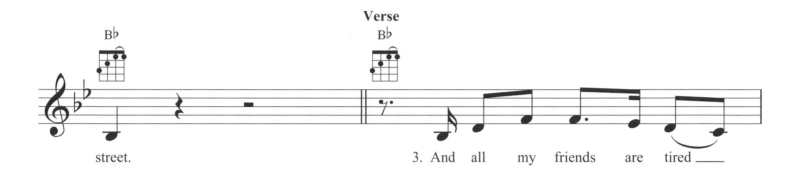

they'll nev - er know you the way that I do. Yeah, to - day I drove through the sub-urbs and

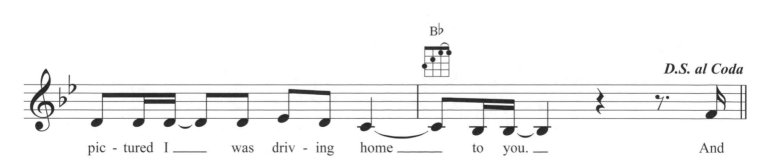

pic - tured I _____ was driv - ing home _____ to you. _____ And

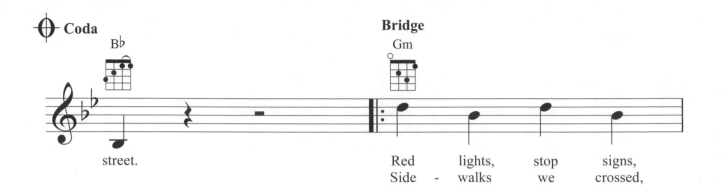

Coda   **Bridge**

B♭   Gm

street.   Red   lights,   stop   signs,
                           Side - walks   we   crossed,

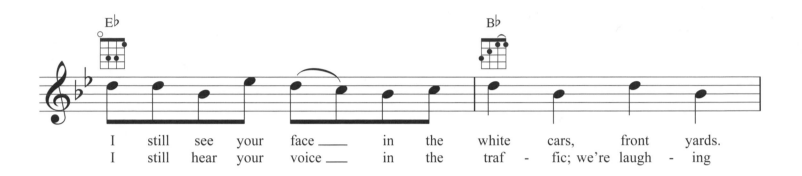

E♭   B♭

I   still   see   your   face ___   in   the   white   cars,   front   yards.
I   still   hear   your   voice ___   in   the   traf - fic; we're   laugh - ing

F   Gm

Can't   drive   past   the   plac - es   we   used   to   go   to,   'cause
o - ver   all   the   noise. ___   God,   I'm   so   blue, know we're   through,   but

E♭   B♭   F

you know   I   still   love   you,   babe. ___
you know   I   still   love   you,   babe. ___

Chorus

E♭

I   know   we   weren't   per - fect,   but   I've   nev - er   felt   this   way   for

no one.   And   I   just   can't   i - mag - ine   how   you

could   be   so   o - kay   now   that   I'm ____ gone.   Guess

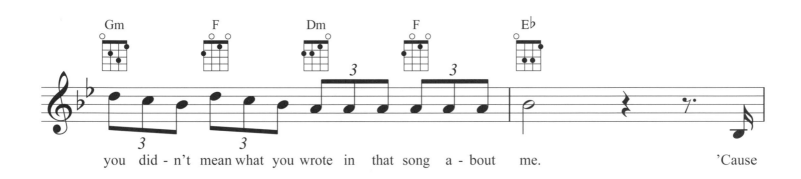

you   did - n't   mean what you wrote in that song a - bout me.   'Cause

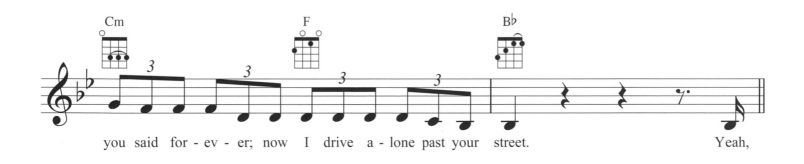

you said for - ev - er; now I drive a - lone past your street.   Yeah,

Outro

you said for - ev - er; now I drive a - lone past your street.

Traitor

Words and Music by Olivia Rodrigo and Daniel Nigro

First note

Verse
Moderate Waltz

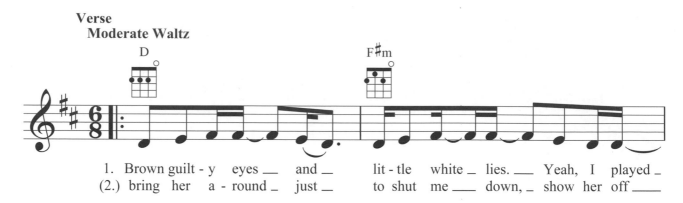

1. Brown guilt-y eyes ___ and ___ lit-tle white ___ lies. ___ Yeah, I played ___
(2.) bring her a-round ___ just ___ to shut me ___ down, ___ show her off ___

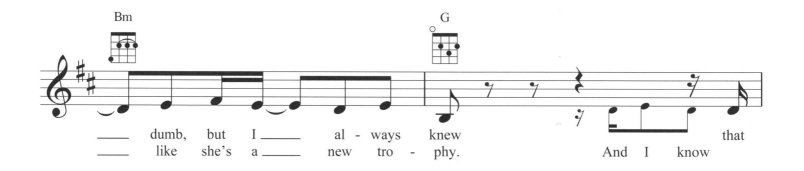

___ dumb, but I ___ al-ways knew   that
___ like she's a ___ new tro-phy.   And I know

you talked to her, ___ may-be did e-ven worse. ___ I kept
if you were true, ___ there's no damn way that you ___ could fall in

qui-et so I ___ could keep you. ___   And ain't it
love with some-bod-y that quick-ly.   Ain't it

fun - ny   how you ran to her _____   the
fun - ny,   all the twist - ed games, _ all the

sec - ond that _____ we called it quits?   And ain't it
ques - tions you _____ used to a - void?   Ain't it

fun - ny   how you said _____ you were friends? _   Now
fun - ny;   re - mem - ber I _____ brought her up _____ and you told _

it sure as _____ hell don't look like it. You be -
_____ me I _____ was par - a - noid?   You be -

𝄋 Chorus

trayed me,   and
trayed me,   and   } I know that you'll nev - er feel _____
trayed me,   'cause

sor - ry for the way I ____ hurt, ____ yeah. ____

You talked to her ____ when we were to - geth - er. { (1., 2.) Loved
{ (D.S.) You

you at your worst, _ }
gave me your word, _ } but that did - n't mat - ter. It

took you two ____ weeks to go off and date ____ her. Guess

To Coda ⊕
N.C.

you did - n't cheat, but you're still a trai - tor. ____

1.
Interlude
D

2.
Bridge
D   F#m

2. Now you   Ah, ____

God, I wish that you had thought this through _ be - fore I went and fell in love with you. _

Ah, _____ when she's sleep-ing in the bed we made, don't you

D.S. al Coda

dare for-get a - bout the way you be -

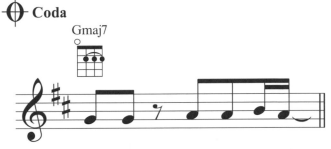

Coda

you're still, you're still a trai -

Outro

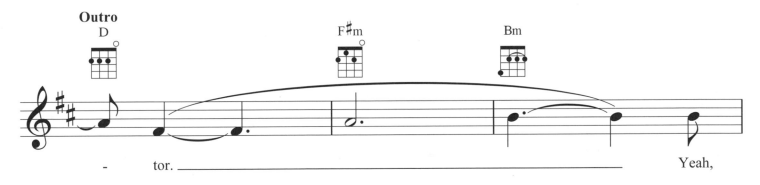

- tor. _____ Yeah,

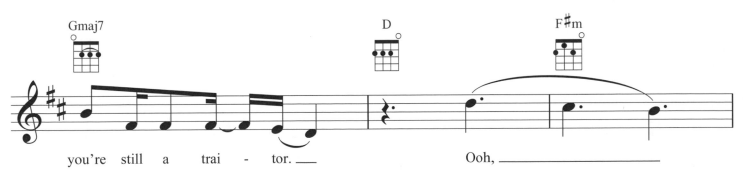

you're still a trai - tor. __ Ooh, _____

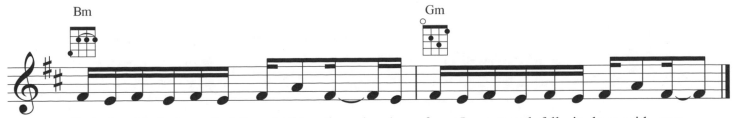

God, I wish that you had thought this through _ be - fore I went and fell in love with you. _

1 Step Forward, 3 Steps Back

Words and Music by Olivia Rodrigo, Jack Antonoff and Taylor Swift

First note

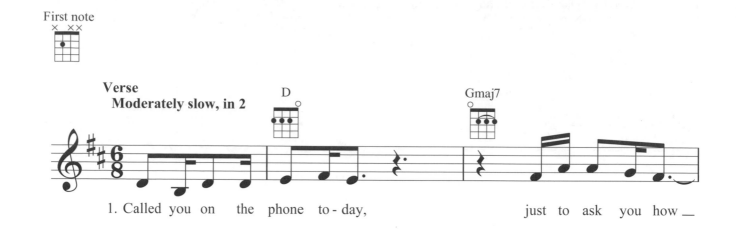

1. Called you on the phone to-day, just to ask you how __ __ you were.

All I did was speak __ nor - mal - ly;

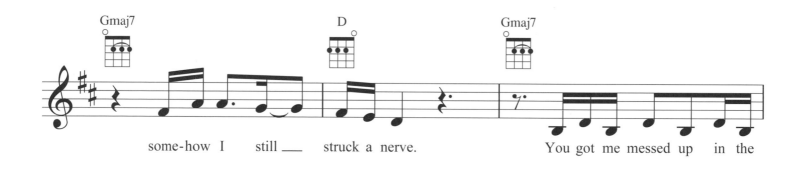

some-how I still __ struck a nerve. You got me messed up in the

head, boy. Nev - er doubt-ed my - self __ so much.

Outro-Chorus

back and forth; _ did I do some-thing wrong? _ It's back and forth; _ may-be

this is all your fault in-stead. It's one step for-ward _ and

three steps _ back. And I'd leave you, but the roll-er coast-er's

all I've ev-er had. Yeah, it's one step for-ward _ and

three steps _ back. _ Do you love me, want me, hate me? Boy, I

don't un-der-stand. _ No, I don't _ un-der-stand. _

Deja Vu

Words and Music by Olivia Rodrigo and Daniel Nigro

First note

Verse
Moderately

1. Car rides ___ to Mal-i-bu, ___ straw-ber-ry ice cream, one

spoon for two, ___ and trad-ing jack-ets, laugh-ing 'bout how small it looks on

you. Watch-ing ___

re-runs of "Glee," ___ be-ing an-noy-ing, sing-ing in har-mo-ny. ___ I bet she's

brag-ging to all her friends, say-ing you're so u-nique.

§ Chorus

So, when you gon-na tell her that we did that, too? __ She thinks it's

spe - cial, but it's all re - used. __ { That was our / That was the

place; I found it first. __ I made the jokes __ you tell to her __ when she's with
show we talked a - bout, __ played you the songs __ she's sing - ing now __ when she's with

To Coda

you. } / you. } Do you get dé - jà vu when she's with you? _____ Do

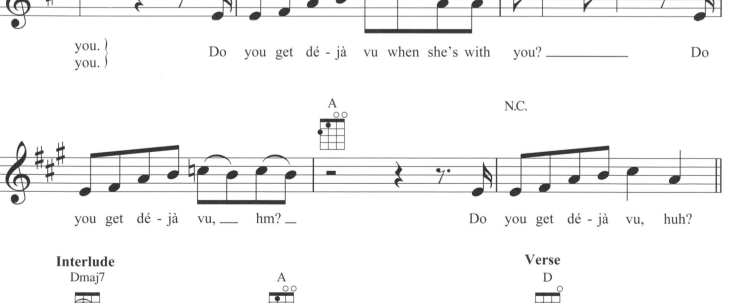

you get dé - jà vu, __ hm? __   Do you get dé - jà vu, huh?

Interlude

Verse

2. Do you call her, ___ al - most

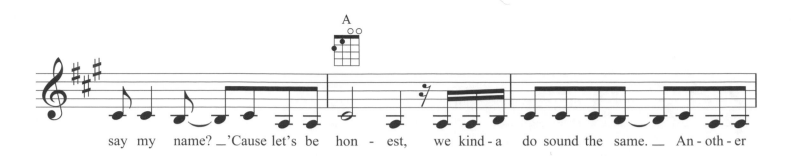

say my name? __'Cause let's be hon - est, we kind-a do sound the same. __ An-oth-er

ac - tress; I hate to think that I was just your type.

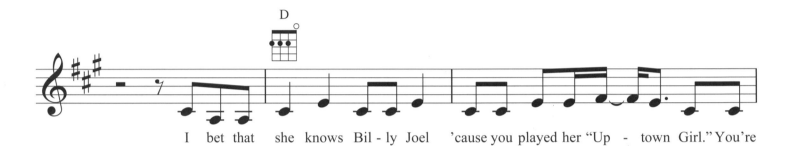

I bet that she knows Bil - ly Joel 'cause you played her "Up - town Girl." You're

sing-ing it to-geth-er now. I bet you e - ven tell her how you love her

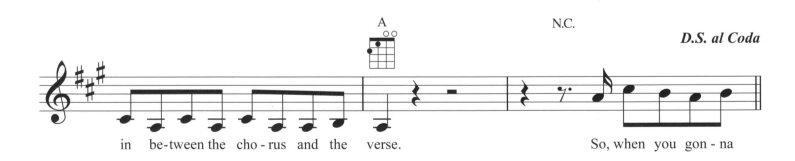

D.S. al Coda

in be-tween the cho-rus and the verse. So, when you gon - na

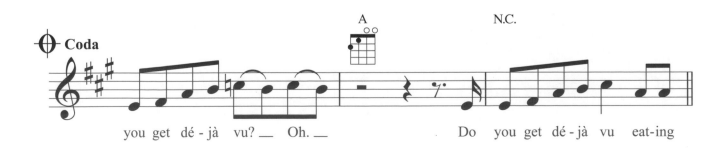

Coda

you get dé-jà vu? __ Oh. __ Do you get dé-jà vu eat-ing

Bridge

straw-ber-ry ice cream in Mal-i-bu? Don't act like we did-n't do all that, too.

You're trad-ing jack-ets like we used to do. (Yeah, ev-'ry-thing is all re-used.)

Play her pi-an-o, but she does-n't know that I was the one who taught you Bil-ly Joel.

A dif-f'rent girl now, but there's noth-ing new. I know you get dé-jà vu.

Outro

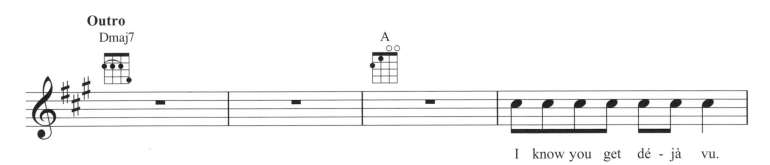

I know you get dé-jà vu.

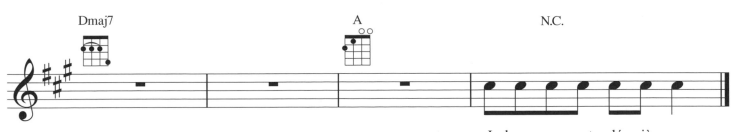

I know you get dé-jà vu.

Good 4 U

Words and Music by Olivia Rodrigo and Daniel Nigro

First note

Verse
Driving Pop Rock

1. Well, good for you, I guess you moved on real-ly eas-i-ly.

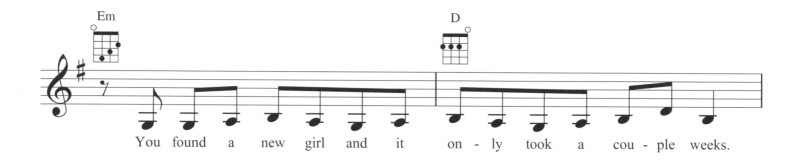

You found a new girl and it on-ly took a cou-ple weeks.

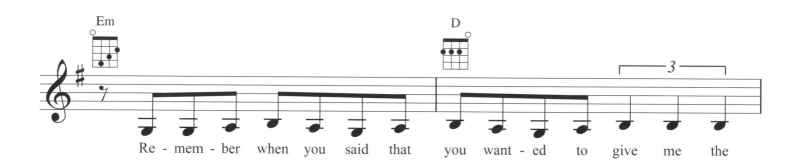

Re-mem-ber when you said that you want-ed to give me the

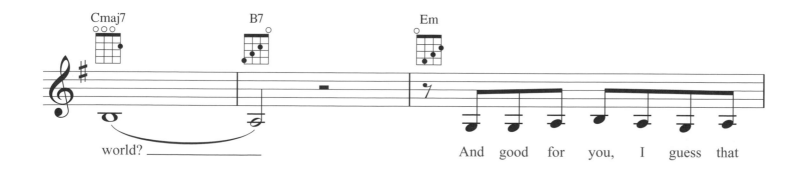

world? _____ And good for you, I guess that

you've been work-ing on your-self. I guess that ther-a-pist I

found for you, she real-ly helped. Now you can be a bet-ter

man ___ for your brand-new girl. ___

𝄋 **Chorus**

Well, good for you, ___ you look hap - py and health-

-y. Not me, if you ev-er cared ___ to ask. ___

{1., 2. Good for you, ___ you're do-ing great out there with-out me, ba-by.
{D.S. Good for you, ___ you're do-ing great out there with-out me, ba-by,

God, I wish that I could do that. _____ } I've lost my
like a damn ___ so - ci - o - path. _____ }

mind, ___ I've spent the night _____ cry - ing on the

floor of my ___ bath - room. _____ But you're so un - af - fect -

- ed, I real - ly don't get it, but I guess

good for you. _____

To Coda 1 ⊕
To Coda 2 ⊕

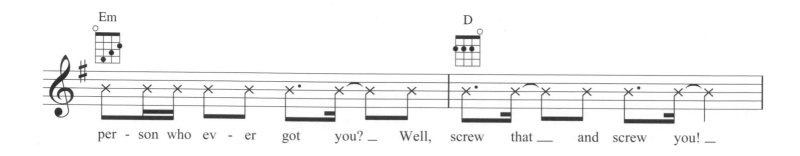

per - son who ev - er got you? _ Well, screw that _ and screw you! _

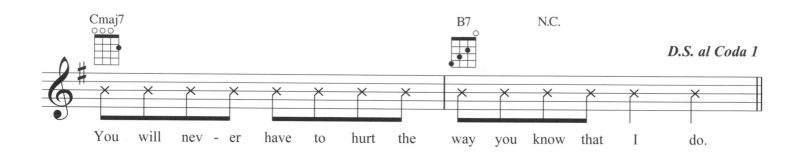

D.S. al Coda 1

You will nev - er have to hurt the way you know that I do.

Interlude

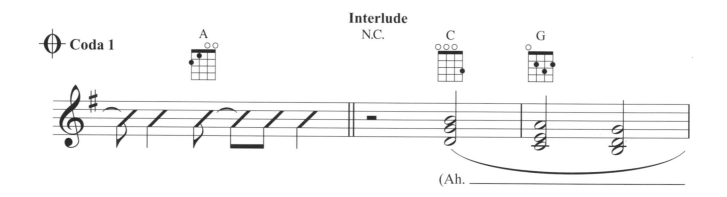

⊕ **Coda 1**

(Ah. _____

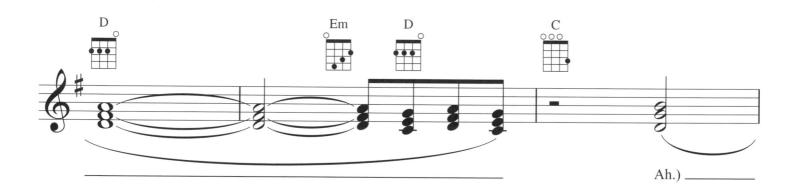

Ah.) _____

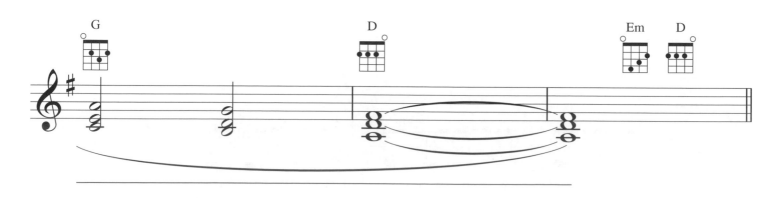

Bridge

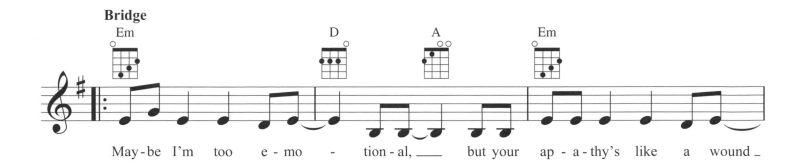

May-be I'm too e-mo - tion-al, ____ but your ap-a-thy's like a wound __

____ in salt. ____ May-be I'm too e-mo - tion-al, ____ or

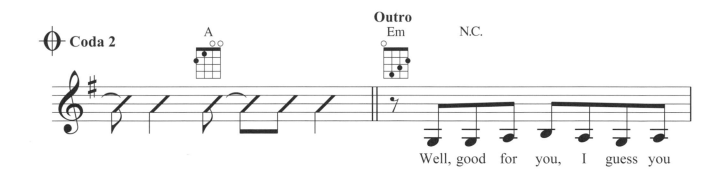

may-be you nev-er cared ___ at all. ____ ___ at all. ___

D.S. al Coda 2

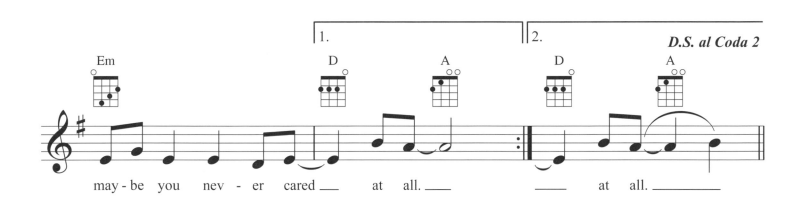

Well, good for you, I guess you

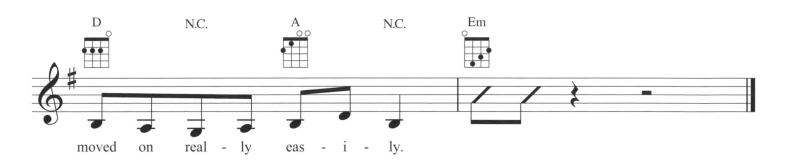

moved on real-ly eas - i - ly.

Enough for You

Words and Music by Olivia Rodrigo

First note

Verse
Moderate Folk, in 2

1. I wore make - up when we dat - ed 'cause I

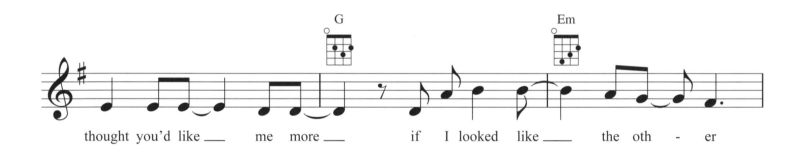

thought you'd like ___ me more ___ if I looked like ___ the oth - er

prom queens I know that you loved ___ be - fore. ___ Tried so

hard to be ___ ev - 'ry - thing that you like, ___ just

for you to say ____ you're not ___ the com - pli - ment

%. Verse

type.

2. And I knew how ___ you took ___ your cof -
3. And may - be I'm ___ just not ___ as in -

- fee and ___ your fa - v'rite songs ___ by heart. I read all ___
- t'rest - ing as the girls ___ you had ___ be - fore. But God, you

____ of your __ self - help ___ books so ___ you'd think that I ___ was smart. _
could - n't have __ cared less ___ a - bout __ some - one who loved _ you more. _

____ Stu - pid, e - mo - tion - al, ___ ob - ses - sive lit - tle me. _
____ I say you broke ___ my heart, _ but you broke much more than that. _

____ I knew from the start ___ this is ___ ex - act -
____ Now I don't want your sym - pa - thy, ___ I just _

all I ev-er want-ed was to be e-nough __ for you. __

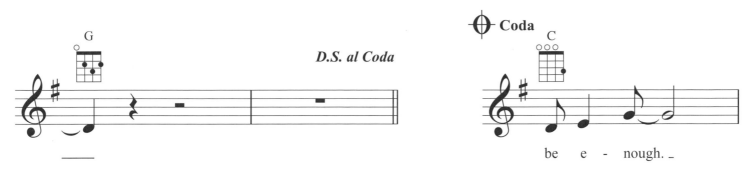

D.S. al Coda

__

Coda

be e-nough. __

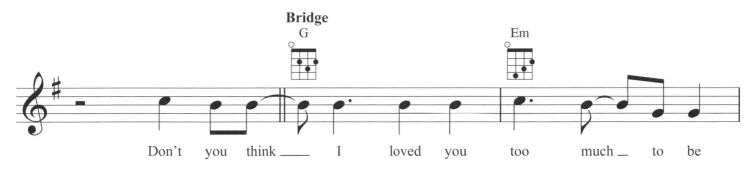

Bridge

Don't you think ___ I loved you too much __ to be

used and ___ dis-card-ed? Don't you think ___ I loved you

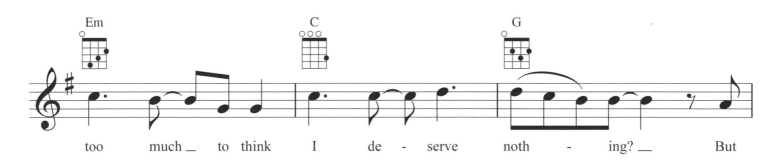

too much __ to think I de-serve noth-ing? __ But

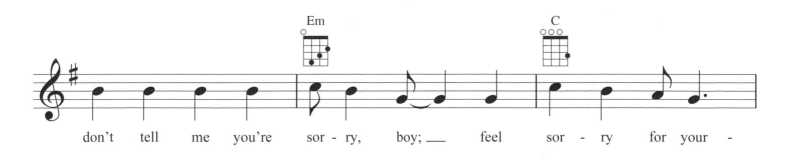

don't tell me you're sor-ry, boy; ___ feel sor-ry for your -

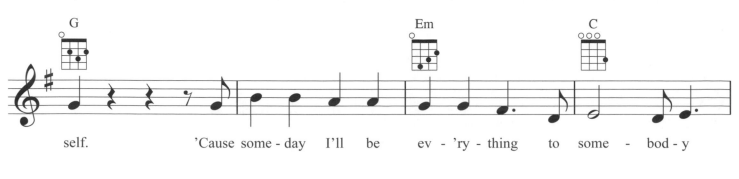

self.   'Cause some - day I'll be ev - 'ry - thing to some - bod - y

Chorus 2

else.   They'll think that I _____ am so ex - cit -

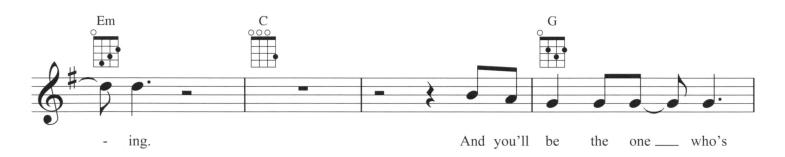

- ing.   And you'll be the one ___ who's

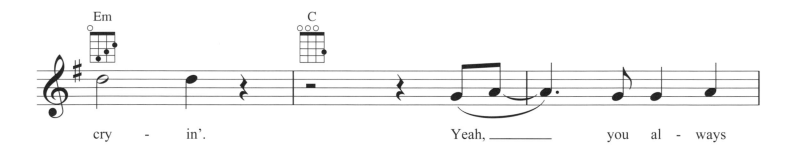

cry - in'.   Yeah, _____ you al - ways

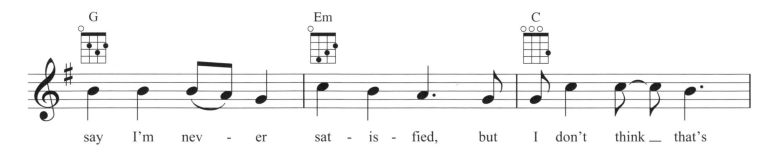

say I'm nev - er sat - is - fied, but I don't think ___ that's

true.   You say I'm nev - er sat - is - fied, but

that's not me, ___ it's you. ___ 'Cause all I ev - er

want - ed was to be e - nough. ___ But I

don't think an - y - thing could ev - er be e - nough ___

Outro

for you, _____ ooh, _____

e - nough ___ for you, oh, _____

___ no, noth - ing's e - nough for you.

Happier

Words and Music by Olivia Rodrigo

First note

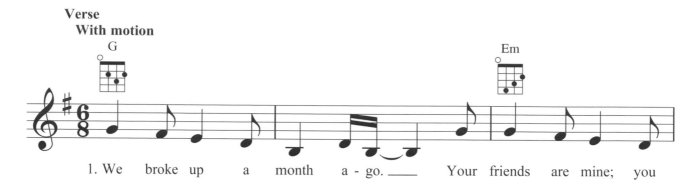

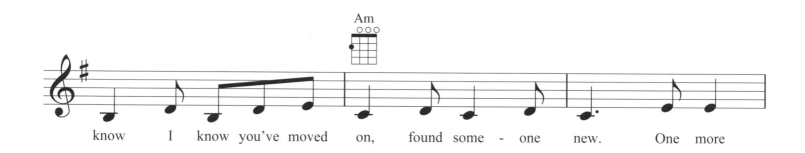

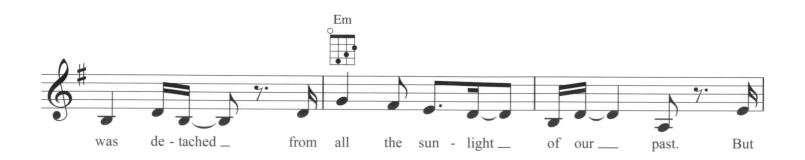

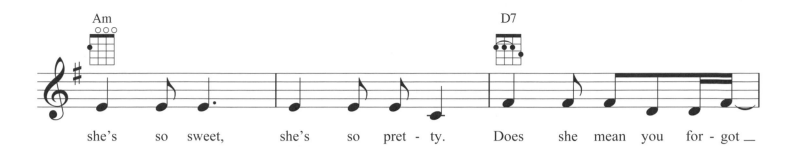

she's so sweet, she's so pret - ty. Does she mean you for - got __

Chorus

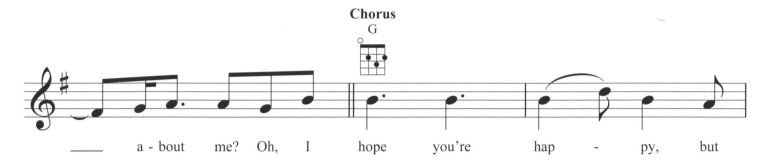

__ a - bout me? Oh, I hope you're hap - py, but

not like how you were with me. I'm self - ish, I know. I

can't let you go. So, find some - one great, but don't find no one bet - ter. __

I hope you're hap - py, but don't be hap - pi - er. __ 2. And

Verse

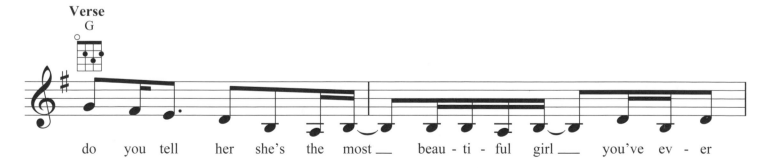

do you tell her she's the most __ beau - ti - ful girl __ you've ev - er

seen, and prom - ise three words you know you'll nev - er

mean? _____ Re - mem - ber when I be - lieved _____ you meant it when you

said it first to me? _____ And now I'm pick - ing _____

her a - part, _____ like cut - ting her _____ down _____ will make you

miss my wretch - ed heart. _____ But she's beau - ti - ful, _____ she looks

kind, she prob - 'ly gives you but - ter - flies. I

Chorus

hope you're hap - py, but not like how you

were with me. I'm self - ish, I know. I can't let you go. So,

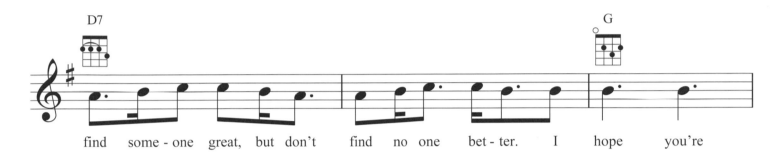

find some - one great, but don't find no one bet - ter. I hope you're

hap - py. I ____ wish you all the best, real - ly. Say

you love her, ba - by, just not like you loved ___ me. And

think of me fond - ly when your ___ hands are on ___ her.

I hope you're hap - py, but don't be hap - pi - er. ____

Interlude

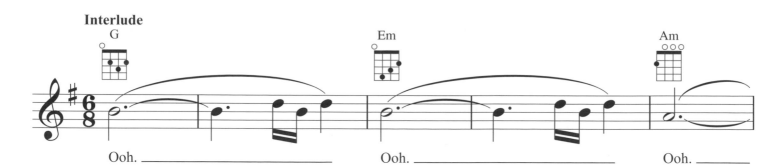

Ooh. _____ Ooh. _____ Ooh. ____

Outro-Chorus

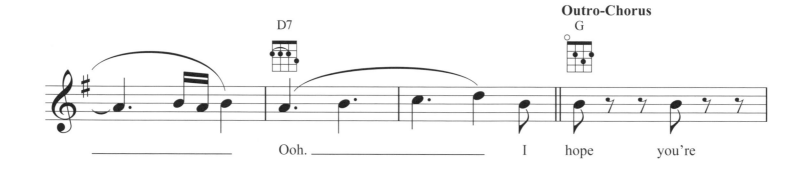

_____ Ooh. _____ I hope you're

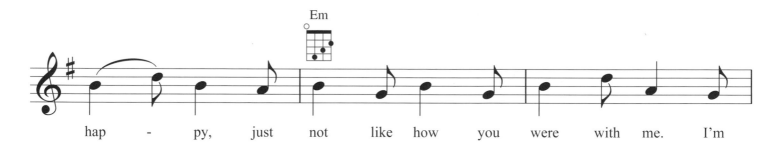

hap - py, just not like how you were with me. I'm

self - ish, I know. Can't let you go. So, find some - one great, but don't

find no one bet - ter. ____ I hope you're hap - py, but don't be hap - pi - er. ____

Jealousy, Jealousy

Words and Music by Olivia Rodrigo, Casey Cathleen Smith and Daniel Nigro

First note

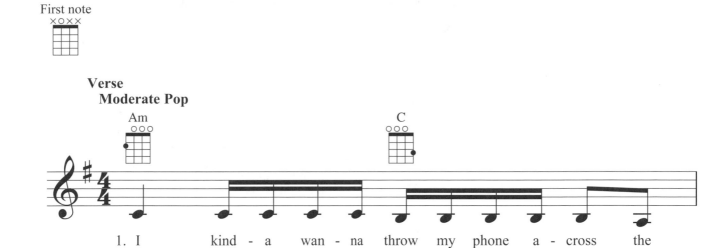

Verse
Moderate Pop

1. I kind-a wan-na throw my phone a-cross the

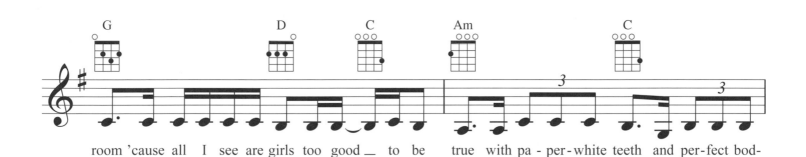

room 'cause all I see are girls too good _ to be true with pa-per-white teeth and per-fect bod-

ies. Wish I did-n't care. _ I know their beau-ty's not my

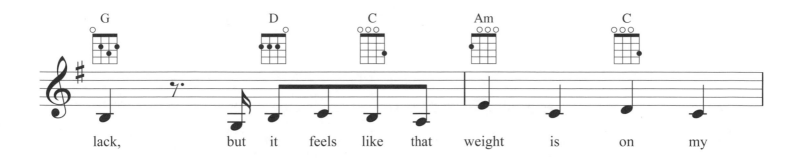

lack, but it feels like that weight is on my

back and I can't let it go. Com- com- par- i - son

com- com- par- i - son is

kill - ing me slow - ly. I think I think too much 'bout

kids who don't know me. I'm so sick of my - self. I'd

rath - er be, rath - er be ___ an - y - one, an - y - one else. My

jeal - ous - y, jeal - ous - y ___ start- ed fol - low- ing ___ me. (He he he ___ he.) ___

___ Start- ed fol - low - ing ___ me. ___ (He he he ___ he.) ___

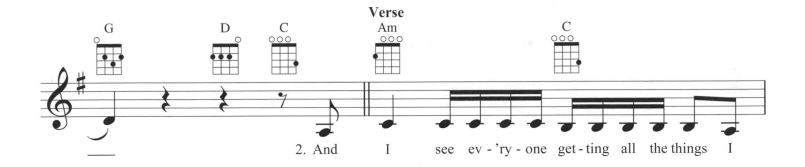

Verse

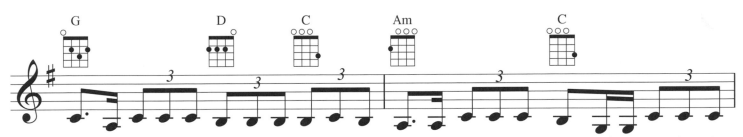

2. And I see ev-'ry-one get-ting all the things I

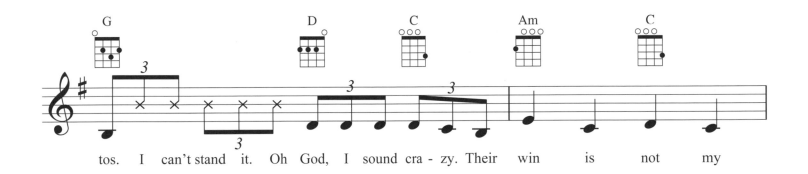

want. I'm hap-py for them, but then a-gain I'm not. Just cool vin-tage clothes and va-ca-tion pho-

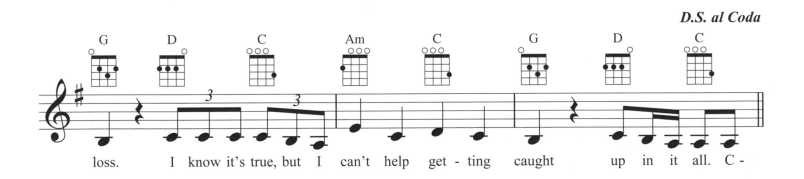

tos. I can't stand it. Oh God, I sound cra-zy. Their win is not my

D.S. al Coda

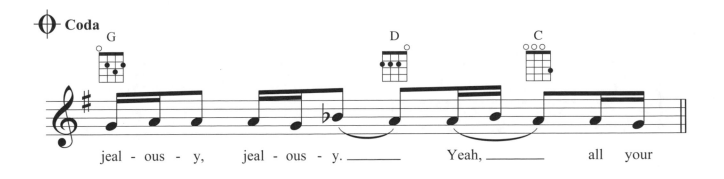

loss. I know it's true, but I can't help get-ting caught up in it all. C-

Coda

jeal-ous-y, jeal-ous-y. Yeah, all your

Bridge

friends are so cool, you go out ev-er-y night ___ in your

dad-dy's nice car. ___ Yeah, you're liv-ing the life. ___ Got a

pret-ty face, ___ a pret-ty boy-friend, too. ___ I wan-na

be you so bad, ___ and I don't e-ven know you.

All I see ___ is what I should be: ___ hap-pi-er, pret-ti-er. Jeal-ous-y, jeal-ous-y.

All I see ___ is what I should be. ___ I'm los-ing it; all I get's jeal-ous-y, jeal-ous-y.

44

Favorite Crime

Words and Music by Olivia Rodrigo and Daniel Nigro

First note

Verse
Moderately, in 2

1. Know that I love you so bad,
(2.) used me as an al - i - bi. I

I let you treat me like that. I was your
crossed my heart as you crossed the line. And I de - fend - ed

will - ing ac - com - plice, hon - ey. _____ And
you ___ to all my friends. _____ And now And

I watched as you fled the scene, ___ doe - eyed as you
ev - 'ry time a si - ren sounds, ___ I won - der if

bur - ied me. ___ One heart broke, four hands
you're a - round. ___ 'Cause you ___ know that I'd do ___ it all a -

Chorus

blood - y. ___ The things ___ I did
gain. ___ All the things ___ I did

just so I could call you

mine. ___ The things ___ you

did. Well, I hope I was your fa - v'rite

1.

crime. ___ 2. You

Bridge

It's bit-ter-sweet to think a-bout the dam-age that we do. 'Cause

I was go-ing down, but I was do-ing it with you. Yeah, ev-'ry-thing we broke and all the

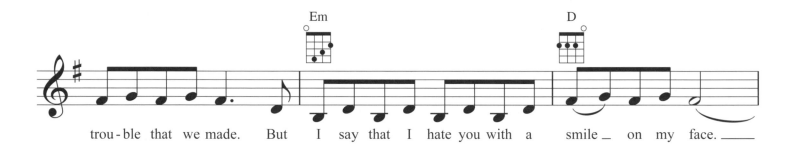

trou-ble that we made. But I say that I hate you with a smile _ on my face. _____

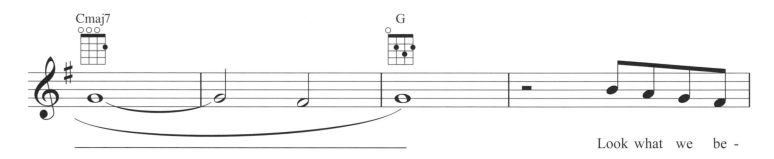

Look what we be -

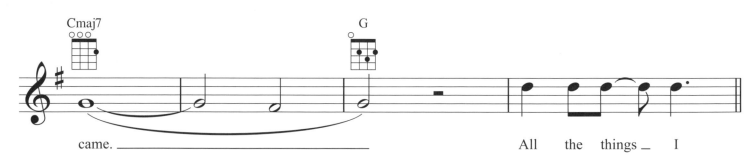

came. _____ All the things _ I

Chorus

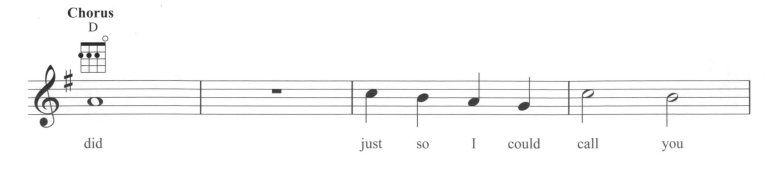

did just so I could call you

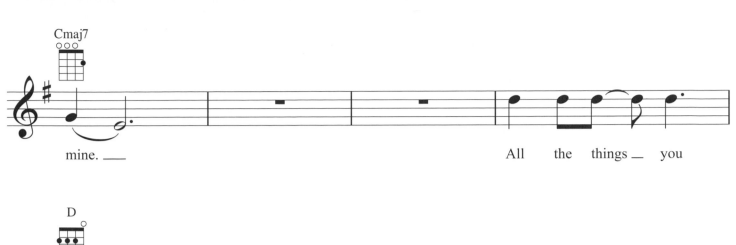

mine. ____

did.   Well,   I   hope   I   was   your

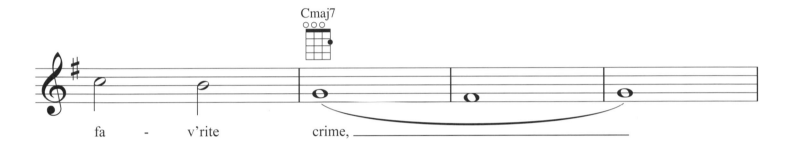

fa - v'rite   crime, _____

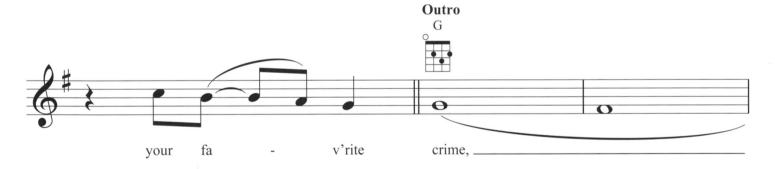

your   fa - v'rite   crime, _____

____   your   fa - v'rite   crime. _____

_____   'Cause, ba - by, you were mine.

Hope Ur OK

Words and Music by Olivia Rodrigo and Daniel Nigro

First note

Verse
Gentle Ballad

1. Knew a boy ___ once when I was small, ___
2. My mid-dle school friend ___ grew up a-lone; ___

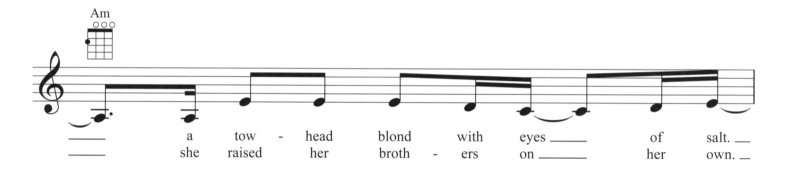

___ a tow-head blond with eyes ___ of salt. ___
___ she raised her broth-ers on ___ her own. ___

___ He played the drum ___ in the march-ing band. ___
___ Her par-ents hat-ed who ___ she loved. ___

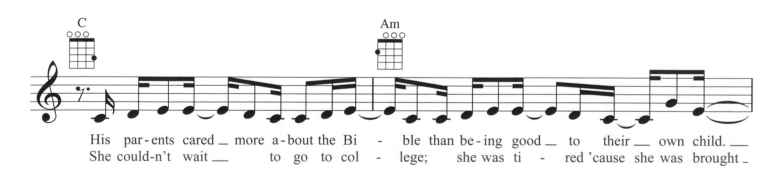

His par-ents cared ___ more a-bout the Bi - ble than be-ing good ___ to their ___ own child. ___
She could-n't wait ___ to go to col-lege; she was ti - red 'cause she was brought ___

C   Am

_____ He wore long   sleeves 'cause of his   dad. __   And
_____ in - to a world __ where   fam - i - ly ____ was mere - ly blood. __   Does she know _

Chorus

F   Am

some - how ____ we fell ____ out ____ of touch.   Hope he took _
_____ how proud I am ____ she was cre - at - ed ____   with the cour -

F   Am

_____ his bad ____ deal and made a roy - al flush.   Don't know _
- age to ____ un - learn ____ all of ____ their ha - tred? _   We don't _

F   Am

_____ if I'll ____ see you ____ a - gain ____ some - day,   but if you're out _
_____ talk much, _ but I've ____ just got ____ to say: I miss _

To Coda ✛   **Interlude**

G   G7   C

_____ there,   I hope that you're _ o - kay. _____
_____ you.

D.C. al Coda

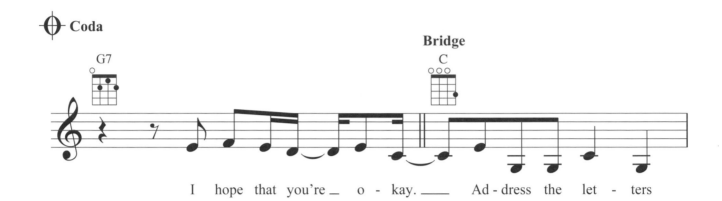

Coda

Bridge

I hope that you're __ o - kay. __ Ad - dress the let - ters

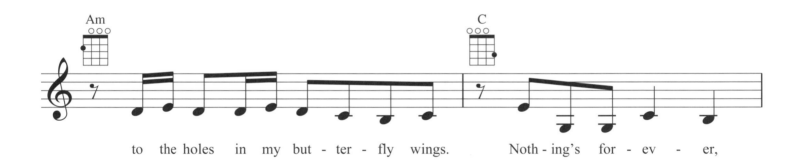

to the holes in my but - ter - fly wings. Noth - ing's for - ev - er,

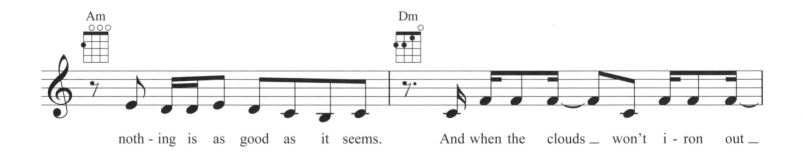

noth - ing is as good as it seems. And when the clouds __ won't i - ron out __

__ and the mon - sters creep in - to your house __ and ev - 'ry door __ is hard to

Outro-Chorus

close,   well, I hope you know ___ how proud ___ I am ___ you were ___ cre - at -

- ed   with the cour - age to un - learn ___ all of their

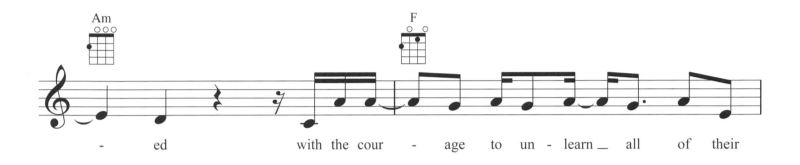

ha - tred. ___   Oh God, I _____ hope that you're hap - pi - er _____ to - day. ___

'Cause I love ___ you,

and I hope that you're ___ o - kay. ___

Ukulele Songbooks

FROM YOUR FAVORITE ARTISTS

The Beatles for Fingerstyle Ukulele

arr. Fred Sokolow

The Beatles for Fingerstyle Ukulele contains 25 favorite songs. Songs include: Across the Universe • Can't Buy Me Love • Eight Days a Week • Here Comes the Sun • Hey Jude • Lucy in the Sky with Diamonds • Yesterday • You've Got to Hide Your Love Away • and more.

00124415 .... $19.99

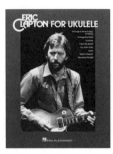

Eric Clapton for Ukulele

18 songs from Slow Hand presented in arrangements with melody, lyrics & chord diagrams for standard G-C-E-A tuning. Includes: Badge • Change the World • Cocaine • I Shot the Sheriff • Lay down Sally • Layla • My Father's Eyes • Sunshine of Your Love • Tears in Heaven • Wonderful Tonight • and more.

00277358 .... $14.99

The Elise Ecklund Songbook

10 cover arrangements for ukulele from internet sensation Elise Ecklund. Includes: Bellyache (Billie Eilish) • Can't Help Falling in Love (Twenty One Pilots) • ME! (Taylor Swift ft. Brandon Urie) • Ocean Eyes (Billie Eilish) • Over the Rainbow (IZ) • Shape of You (Ed Sheeran) • and more.

00319563 .... $9.99

Grateful Dead for Ukulele

Now Dead Heads can strum along to 20 of their favorites on the ukulele! Songs include: Box of Rain • Brokedown Palace • Casey Jones • Friend of the Devil • The Golden Road • Ripple • Sugar Magnolia • Touch of Grey • Truckin' • Uncle John's Band • and more.

00139464 .... $12.99

Bob Marley for Ukulele

Ya mon! 20 Marley favorites to strum on your uke, including: Buffalo Soldier • Could You Be Loved • Exodus • Get Up Stand Up • I Shot the Sheriff • Jamming • Lively Up Yourself • No Woman No Cry • One Love • Redemption Song • Stir It Up • Three Little Birds • and more.

00129925 .... $15.99

Tom Petty for Ukulele

Get ready to strum, sing and pick along with 17 Tom Petty tunes! Includes: American Girl • Breakdown • Don't Come Around Here No More • Don't Do Me Like That • Free Fallin' • Learning to Fly • Mary Jane's Last Dance • Runnin' Down a Dream • Wildflowers • You Don't Know How It Feels • and more.

00192241 .... $14.99

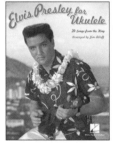

Elvis Presley for Ukulele

arr. Jim Beloff

Strum, sing and pick along with 20 classic hits from The King, expertly arranged for ukulele by Jim Beloff. Includes: All Shook Up • Blue Suede Shoes • Can't Help Falling in Love • Heartbreak Hotel • Hound Dog • Jailhouse Rock • Love Me • Love Me Tender • Suspicious Minds • Teddy Bear • and more.

00701004 .... $15.99

Queen for Ukulele

14 hits from Freddie Mercury and crew for uke. Includes: Another One Bites the Dust • Bohemian Rhapsody • Crazy Little Thing Called Love • Don't Stop Me Now • I Want It All • I Want to Break Free • Killer Queen • Radio Ga Ga • Save Me • The Show Must Go On • Under Pressure • We Are the Champions • We Will Rock You • You're My Best Friend.

00218304 .... $14.99

Jake Shimabukuro – Peace Love Ukulele

Deemed "the Hendrix of the ukulele," Hawaii native Jake Shimabukuro is a uke virtuoso whose music has revolutionized the world's perception of this tiny instrument. Songs include: Bohemian Rhapsody • Boy Meets Girl • Hallelujah • and more.

00702516 .... $19.99

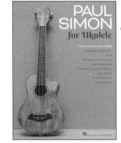

Paul Simon for Ukulele

Strum your favorite Simon songs on the ukulele with this collection of 17 songs, including: Bridge Over Troubled Water • Cecilia • Loves Me like a Rock • Me and Julio down by the Schoolyard • Mrs. Robinson • The Sound of Silence • You Can Call Me Al • and more.

00280905 .... $14.99

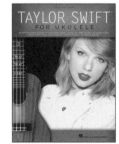

Taylor Swift for Ukulele – 2nd Edition

This second edition has been updated to include selections through 1989 for a total of 20 Swift hits, featuring: Bad Blood • Blank Space • I Knew You Were Trouble • Mean • Shake It Off • Teardrops on My Guitar • Wildest Dreams • You Belong with Me • and more.

00702544 .... $16.99

Grace Vanderwaal – Just the Beginning

13-year-old ukulele player and singer-songwriter Grace VanderWaal's ukulele songbook features all 12 songs from her debut album: A Better Life • Burned • City Song • I Don't Know My Name • Insane Sometimes • Just a Crush • Moonlight • Sick of Being Told • and more.

00261512 .... $14.99

Order these and more songbooks from your favorite music retailer at **halleonard.com**

The Best Collections for Ukulele

The Best Songs Ever

70 songs have now been arranged for ukulele. Includes: Always • Bohemian Rhapsody • Memory • My Favorite Things • Over the Rainbow • Piano Man • What a Wonderful World • Yesterday • You Raise Me Up • and more.

00282413 . . . . $17.99

Campfire Songs for Ukulele

30 favorites to sing as you roast marshmallows and strum your uke around the campfire. Includes: God Bless the U.S.A. • Hallelujah • The House of the Rising Sun • I Walk the Line • Puff the Magic Dragon • Wagon Wheel • You Are My Sunshine • and more.

00129170 . . . . $14.99

The Daily Ukulele

arr. Liz and Jim Beloff
Strum a different song everyday with easy arrangements of 365 of your favorite songs in one big songbook! Includes favorites by the Beatles, Beach Boys, and Bob Dylan, folk songs, pop songs, kids' songs, Christmas carols, and Broadway and Hollywood tunes, all with a spiral binding for ease of use.

00240356 Original Edition $39.99
00240681 Leap Year Edition $39.99
00119270 Portable Edition $37.50

Disney Hits for Ukulele

Play 23 of your favorite Disney songs on your ukulele. Includes: The Bare Necessities • Cruella De Vil • Do You Want to Build a Snowman? • Kiss the Girl • Lava • Let It Go • Once upon a Dream • A Whole New World • and more.

00151250 . . . . $16.99

Also available:
00291547 **Disney Fun Songs for Ukulele** . . . $16.99
00701708 **Disney Songs for Ukulele** $14.99
00334696 **First 50 Disney Songs on Ukulele** . $16.99

First 50 Songs You Should Play on Ukulele

An amazing collec-tion of 50 accessible, must-know favorites: Edelweiss • Hey, Soul Sister • I Walk the Line • I'm Yours • Imagine • Over the Rainbow • Peaceful Easy Feeling • The Rainbow Connection • Riptide • more.

00149250 . . . . $16.99

Also available:
00292082 **First 50 Melodies on Ukulele** . . . $15.99
00289029 **First 50 Songs on Solo Ukulele** . . $15.99
00347437 **First 50 Songs to Strum on Uke** . $16.99

40 Most Streamed Songs for Ukulele

40 top hits that sound great on uke! Includes: Despacito • Feel It Still • Girls like You • Happier • Havana • High Hopes • The Middle • Perfect • 7 Rings • Shallow • Shape of You • Something Just like This • Stay • Sucker • Sunflower • Sweet but Psycho • Thank U, Next • There's Nothing Holdin' Me Back • Without Me • and more!

00298113 . . . . $17.99

The 4 Chord Songbook

With just 4 chords, you can play 50 hot songs on your ukulele! Songs include: Brown Eyed Girl • Do Wah Diddy Diddy • Hey Ya! • Ho Hey • Jessie's Girl • Let It Be • One Love • Stand by Me • Toes • With or Without You • and many more.

00142050 . . . . $16.99

Also available:
00141143 **The 3-Chord Songbook** $16.99

Pop Songs for Kids

30 easy pop favorites for kids to play on uke, including: Brave • Can't Stop the Feeling! • Feel It Still • Fight Song • Happy • Havana • House of Gold • How Far I'll Go • Let It Go • Remember Me (Ernesto de la Cruz) • Rewrite the Stars • Roar • Shake It Off • Story of My Life • What Makes You Beautiful • and more.

00284415 . . . . $16.99

Simple Songs for Ukulele

50 favorites for standard G-C-E-A ukulele tuning, including: All Along the Watchtower • Can't Help Falling in Love • Don't Worry, Be Happy • Ho Hey • I'm Yours • King of the Road • Sweet Home Alabama • You Are My Sunshine • and more.

00156815 . . . . $14.99

Also available:
00276644 **More Simple Songs for Ukulele** . $14.99

Top Hits of 2020

18 uke-friendly tunes of 2020 are featured in this collection of melody, lyric and chord arrangements in standard G-C-E-A tuning. Includes: Adore You (Harry Styles) • Before You Go (Lewis Capaldi) • Cardigan (Taylor Swift) • Daisies (Katy Perry) • I Dare You (Kelly Clarkson) • Level of Concern (twenty one pilots) • No Time to Die (Billie Eilish) • Rain on Me (Lady Gaga feat. Ariana Grande) • Say So (Doja Cat) • and more.

00355553 . . . . $14.99

Also available:
00302274 **Top Hits of 2019** $14.99

Ukulele: The Most Requested Songs

Strum & Sing Series
Cherry Lane Music
Nearly 50 favorites all expertly arranged for ukulele! Includes: Bubbly • Build Me Up, Buttercup • Cecilia • Georgia on My Mind • Kokomo • L-O-V-E • Your Body Is a Wonderland • and more.

02501453 . . . . $14.99

The Ultimate Ukulele Fake Book

Uke enthusiasts will love this giant, spiral-bound collection of over 400 songs for uke! Includes: Crazy • Dancing Queen • Downtown • Fields of Gold • Happy • Hey Jude • 7 Years • Summertime • Thinking Out Loud • Thriller • Wagon Wheel • and more.

00175500 9" x 12" Edition $45.00
00319997 5.5" x 8.5" Edition $39.99

HAL•LEONARD®

Order today from your favorite music retailer at
halleonard.com

Prices, contents and availability subject to change without notice

Disney characters and artwork TM & © 2021 Disney

0621
479

HAL•LEONARD® UKULELE PLAY-ALONG

AUDIO ACCESS INCLUDED

Now you can play your favorite songs on your uke with great-sounding backing tracks to help you sound like a bona fide pro! The audio also features playback tools so you can adjust the tempo without changing the pitch and loop challenging parts.

1. POP HITS
00701451 Book/CD Pack $15.99

2. UKE CLASSICS
00701452 Book/CD Pack $15.99

3. HAWAIIAN FAVORITES
00701453 Book/Online Audio $14.99

4. CHILDREN'S SONGS
00701454 Book/Online Audio $14.99

5. CHRISTMAS SONGS
00701696 Book/CD Pack $12.99

6. LENNON & McCARTNEY
00701723 Book/Online Audio $12.99

7. DISNEY FAVORITES
00701724 Book/Online Audio $12.99

8. CHART HITS
00701745 Book/CD Pack $15.99

9. THE SOUND OF MUSIC
00701784 Book/CD Pack $14.99

10. MOTOWN
00701964 Book/CD Pack $12.99

11. CHRISTMAS STRUMMING
00702458 Book/Online Audio $12.99

12. BLUEGRASS FAVORITES
00702584 Book/CD Pack $12.99

13. UKULELE SONGS
00702599 Book/CD Pack $12.99

14. JOHNNY CASH
00702615 Book/CD Pack $15.99

15. COUNTRY CLASSICS
00702834 Book/CD Pack $12.99

16. STANDARDS
00702835 Book/CD Pack $12.99

17. POP STANDARDS
00702836 Book/CD Pack $12.99

18. IRISH SONGS
00703086 Book/Online Audio $12.99

19. BLUES STANDARDS
00703087 Book/CD Pack $12.99

20. FOLK POP ROCK
00703088 Book/CD Pack $12.99

21. HAWAIIAN CLASSICS
00703097 Book/CD Pack $12.99

22. ISLAND SONGS
00703098 Book/CD Pack $12.99

23. TAYLOR SWIFT – 2ND EDITION
00221966 Book/Online Audio $16.99

24. WINTER WONDERLAND
00101871 Book/CD Pack $12.99

25. GREEN DAY
00110398 Book/CD Pack $14.99

26. BOB MARLEY
00110399 Book/Online Audio $14.99

27. TIN PAN ALLEY
00116358 Book/CD Pack $12.99

28. STEVIE WONDER
00116736 Book/CD Pack $14.99

29. OVER THE RAINBOW & OTHER FAVORITES
00117076 Book/Online Audio $14.99

30. ACOUSTIC SONGS
00122336 Book/CD Pack $14.99

31. JASON MRAZ
00124166 Book/CD Pack $14.99

32. TOP DOWNLOADS
00127507 Book/CD Pack $14.99

33. CLASSICAL THEMES
00127892 Book/Online Audio $14.99

34. CHRISTMAS HITS
00128602 Book/CD Pack $14.99

35. SONGS FOR BEGINNERS
00129009 Book/Online Audio $14.99

36. ELVIS PRESLEY HAWAII
00138199 Book/Online Audio $14.99

37. LATIN
00141191 Book/Online Audio $14.99

38. JAZZ
00141192 Book/Online Audio $14.99

39. GYPSY JAZZ
00146559 Book/Online Audio $14.99

40. TODAY'S HITS
00160845 Book/Online Audio $14.99

Prices, contents, and availability subject to change without notice.

HAL•LEONARD®

www.halleonard.com